CATDOG™

JOKE BOOK

Based on the TV series *CatDog*®
created by Peter Hannan as seen on Nickelodeon®

Editorial Consultants: Peter Hannan and Robert Lamoreaux
Additional assistance provided by the CatDog Production Team.

SIMON SPOTLIGHT
An imprint of Simon & Schuster Children's Publishing Division
1230 Avenue of the Americas, New York, New York 10020

Produced by Bumpy Slide Books
Designed by sheena needham • ess design and development
Manufactured in the United States of America

First Edition   10 9 8 7 6 5 4 3 2 1

ISBN 0-689-83003-3

CAT DOG™

JOKE BOOK

Simon Spotlight/
Nickelodeon

by Annie Auerbach

What would you get if a row of 120 rabbits took one step backwards?
A receding hare line.

When does CatDog go to a baseball game?
When it's a double-header.

Dog: What's worse than liver?
Cat: What?
Dog: Liverwurst.

What does Cat call it when he burps up a taco?
Dog's lunch.

What do you step in when it rains Shriek and her relatives?
Poodles.

Why did Cat cross the road?
Because Dog was chasing a squirrel.

When is the vet busiest?
When it rains cats and dogs.

What do cats and dogs have in common?
The letter "s."

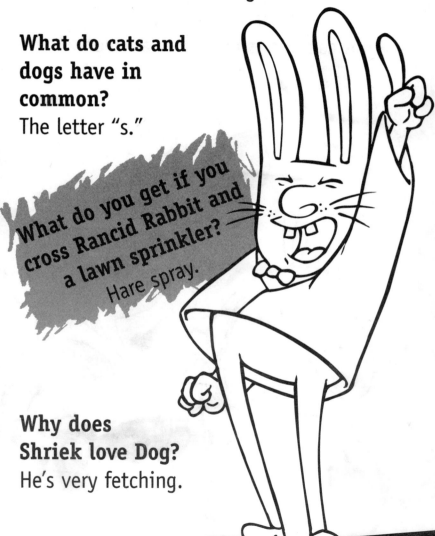

What do you get if you cross Rancid Rabbit and a lawn sprinkler?
Hare spray.

Why does Shriek love Dog?
He's very fetching.

What do you get if you cross a hungry cat and a canary?
A cat who isn't hungry anymore.

Knock, knock.

Who's there?

Anita.

Anita who?

What do you call the trash that Cat tosses on the ground?
Kitty litter.

Why does Cat cough up furballs?
He loves a good gag.

Anita snack. Let's eat!

Why couldn't Dog talk?
Cat got his tongue.

How does Cat swim?
By Dog paddling.

What is Winslow's favorite cereal?
Cream of wit.

Why did Winslow want to move?
He was tired of living in a hole in the wall.

What's worse than raining cats and dogs?

Hailing elephants.

What does Cat love to read?
Catalogs.

11

Why did Cliff put a firecracker under his pancakes?

He wanted to blow his stack.

What is cat fur?

Fur chasing mice.

Why was the mother flea so sad? Because her children were going to the dogs.

13

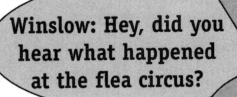

Winslow: Hey, did you hear what happened at the flea circus?

Winslow: CatDog came along and stole the show!

Randolph: No, what happened?

How does Dog like to travel?
On a mutt-a-cycle.

Why did Dog look in Cat's mouth?
To see if there was any money in the kitty.

**What's the best way to catch
Eddie the Squirrel?**
Climb a tree and act like a nut.

How can you say rabbit without using the letter R?
Bunny.

How does Dog spell paradise?
G-A-R-B-A-G-E T-R-U-C-K

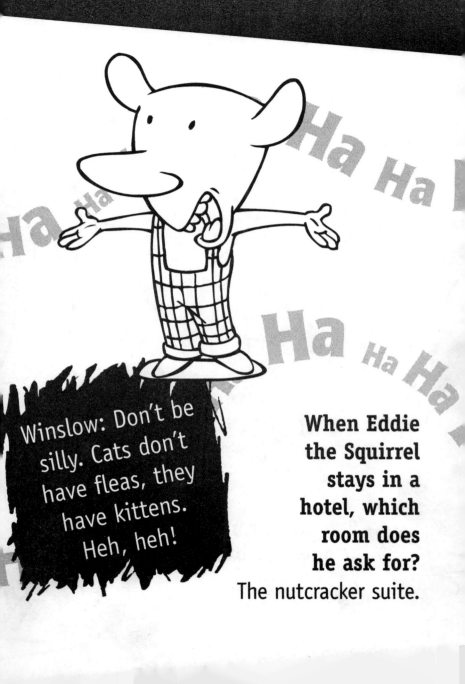

Winslow: Don't be silly. Cats don't have fleas, they have kittens. Heh, heh!

When Eddie the Squirrel stays in a hotel, which room does he ask for? The nutcracker suite.

What does Dog have in common with a tree?
They both have barks.

What are Lube's clothes made of?
Mutt-terial.

Cat: What can you never have for breakfast?
Dog: What?
Cat: Lunch and dinner.

What kind of car does Cat hope to have?
A Cat-o-lac.

What kind of car does Rancid Rabbit drive?

A hop rod.

What's the best way to talk to the Greasers? Long distance.

Shriek: **Knock, knock.**

Lube: Who's there?

Shriek: **Howard.**

Lube: Howard who?

Shriek: **Howard you like to stand out here while someone asks "who's there?"**

Cat: Knock, knock.

Dog: Who's there?

Cat: Run

What did Dog say as he gobbled a frankfurter?
"It's a dog-eat-dog world."

What happened when the cat swallowed a ball of yarn?
She had mittens.

What do you call someone who steals a kitty and then falls asleep?
A catnapping catnapper.

How do you find Dog if he's lost in the woods?
Put your ear to a tree and listen to the bark.

What did Elvis sing to Dog at the shelter?

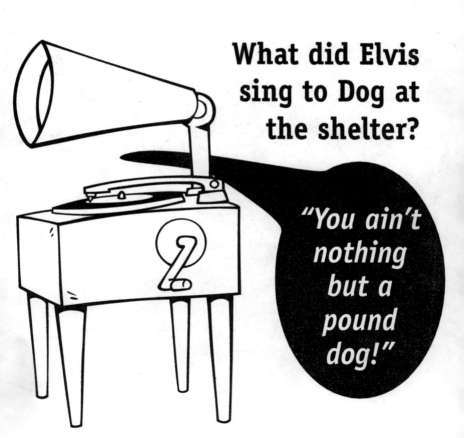

"You ain't nothing but a pound dog!"

When is it bad luck to have a black cat follow you?
When you're a mouse.

**What do you get when Cat
eats a lemon?**
A sour puss.

Spell mousetrap with three letters.
C-A-T.

**When a pretty feline comes along,
what does Cat do?**
He makes a catcall.

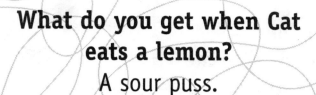

Why does Winslow like the letter S? It makes Cat *scat*!

Why was Cat near the pond?
He was hungry for catfish.

What's the difference between Cat and a frog?
Cat has nine lives, but a frog croaks all the time.

When is Dog not a dog?
When he makes a pig of himself.

How is cat food sold?
A few ounces purr can.

How did Dog get rid of ticks?
By taking off his watch.

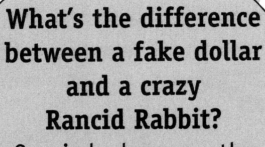

What's the difference between a fake dollar and a crazy Rancid Rabbit?
One is bad money, the other is a mad bunny.

How does Rancid Rabbit travel?
By *hare*plane.

What's Cliff's favorite Mexican food?
Machos.

What does Winslow become when he gets caught in the cold?
A mice cube.

What do you call someone who steals cats?
A purr-snatcher.

What did the teacher do with the naughty cat?
Made him sit in the kitty-corner.

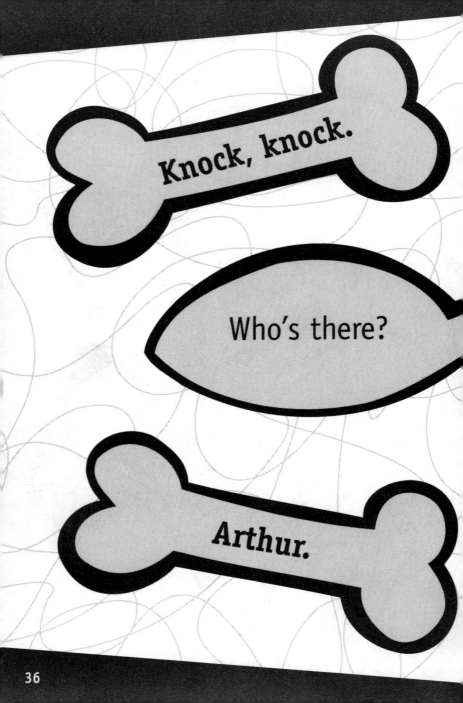

Knock, knock.

Who's there?

Arthur.

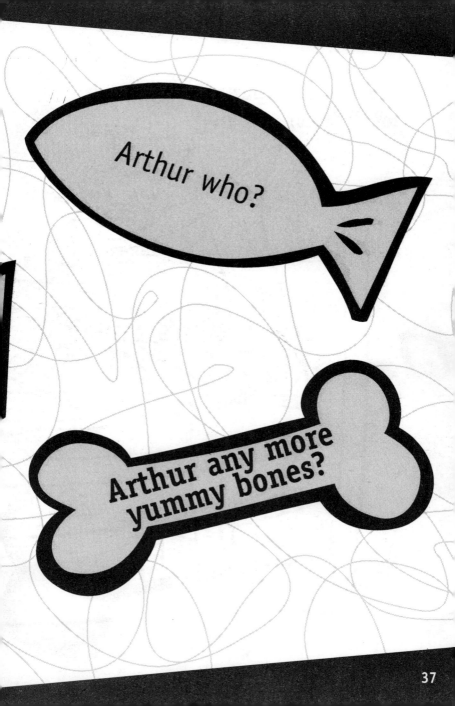

What does Cat put on french fries?

Catsup.

How does Dog like his eggs cooked?
Pooched.

**What does Dog like
to eat for lunch?**
Nearburgers.

Where does CatDog hate to shop?
The flea market.

What kind of dog doesn't bark?
A hot dog.

**What does Cat say
when he stubs his toe?**
Me-owch!

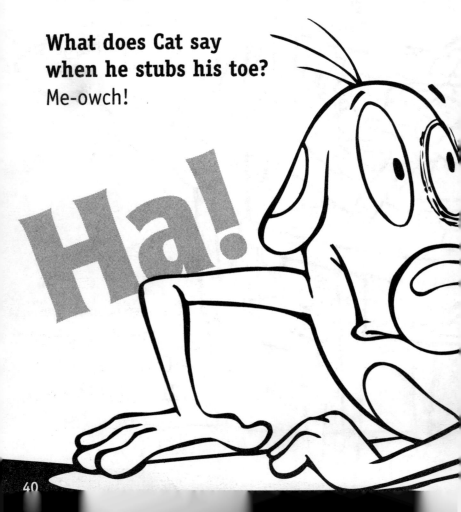

Cliff: Knock, knock.
Cat: Who's there?
Cliff: Radio.
Cat: Radio who?
Cliff: Radio not, here I come!

Why couldn't
Shriek catch
her tail?
Because it's hard to
make ends meet.

Why does Dog scratch himself?
Because Cat won't do it for him.

Why did Dog bite Cat?
Because Cat said Dog should try catnip.

What is the difference between CatDog and a flea?
CatDog can have fleas but a flea can't have CatDogs.

Ha Ha Ha Ha

What is blue and has a trunk?
Winslow going on vacation.

What do you put on top of a doghouse?
A woof.

**What does someone need to know
before teaching tricks to a dog?**
More than the dog.

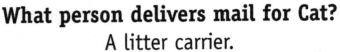

What person delivers mail for Cat?
A litter carrier.

Dog: Knock, knock.
Cat: Who's there?
Dog: Ken.
Cat: Ken who?
Dog: Ken I please eat this pile of garbage?

Where does Rancid Rabbit get his hair cut?
At the hare dresser.

How does a dog buy bones?
By the pound.